Heaven
& HELL

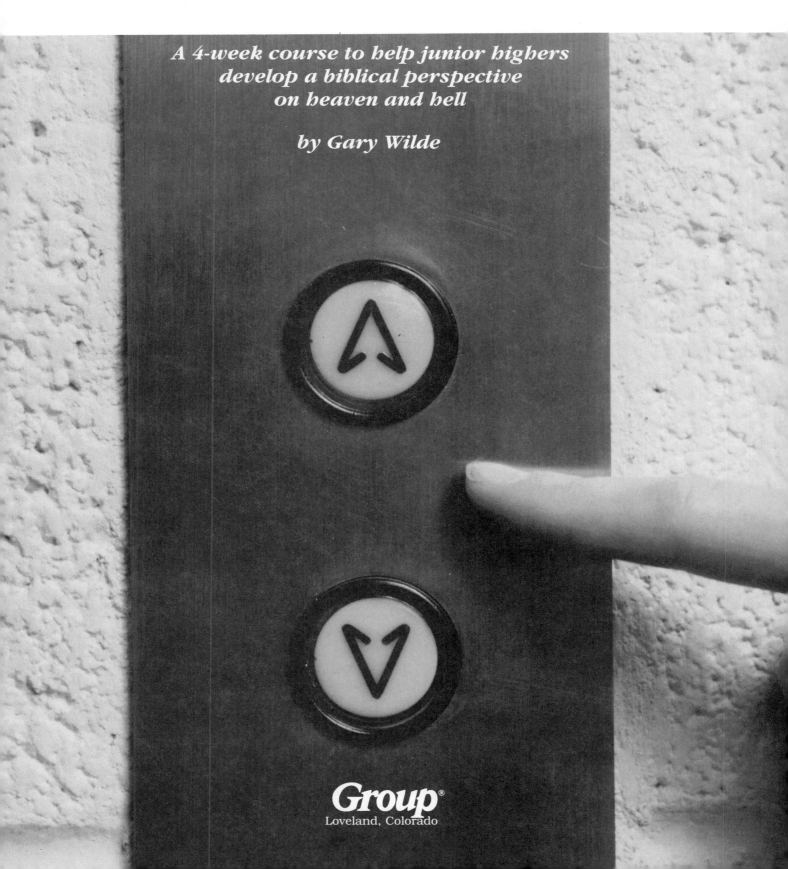

A 4-week course to help junior highers develop a biblical perspective on heaven and hell

by Gary Wilde

Group
Loveland, Colorado

Group®

Credits
Edited by Michael Warden
Cover designed by Jill Nordbye and DeWain Stoll
Interior designed by Judy Bienick and Jan Aufdemberge
Illustrations by Raymond Medici
Cover photo by David Priest

ISBN 1-55945-131-9
Printed in the United States of America.

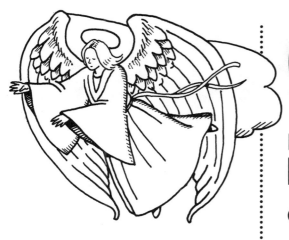

CONTENTS

HEAVEN & HELL

You might think: Why would a teenager care about what life is like in heaven? It's hard enough just figuring out what life is supposed to be like here on Earth!

Perhaps the fact that life is tough for today's teenagers is a good reason to point to life's deeper meaning. It's clear that kids are searching for meaning beyond the everyday. Pick up just about any secular album and you'll find spiritual themes, if not outright depictions of the hellish and demonic. With more than just albums, the afterlife is a popular teenage fare.

But now that popular culture has had its say, what about the church? What are we telling kids about the spiritual realm? What about the biblical teachings on heaven and hell? Kids can benefit from a balanced biblical approach to the spiritual realities of heaven and hell. They can develop their own beliefs— based on scripture— about what heaven and hell are like.

We can also offer kids truths the world tends to overlook. We can give kids hope by showing them heaven is ahead. Not a fake, anemic pie-in-the-sky fantasy world, but the real, spiritual realm God has prepared for those who follow Christ.

Teenagers all want answers to three basic questions: Who am I? Why am I here? and Where am I going? Your kids will be encouraged by the clear pronouncement of Jesus found in

Who's Thinking About Eternity?

According to a recent Gallup poll:

● 78 percent of the general public believe in a heaven where people who have been "good" in their earthly lives are rewarded.

● 60 percent believe in a hell where "bad" people will be punished for eternity.

Of those who claimed no religious belief, there was still a significant belief in life after death:

● 46 percent believe in heaven.

● 34 percent believe in hell.

these lessons: "I am going to prepare a place for you. And I will come again and bring you home."

By the end of this course, your students will:
- discover the Bible's description of heaven;
- examine their feelings about punishment for wrongdoing;
- explore what hell might be;
- consider who gets into heaven;
- be challenged to live as citizens of heaven; and
- understand personally what God requires for them to enter heaven.

COURSE OBJECTIVES

HOW TO USE THIS COURSE

Think back on an important lesson you've learned in life. Did you learn it from reading about it? from hearing about it? from something you experienced? Chances are, the most important lessons you've learned came from something you've experienced. That's what active learning is— learning by doing. And active learning is a key element in Group's Active Bible Curriculum.

Active learning leads students in doing things that help them understand important principles, messages and ideas. It's a discovery process that helps kids internalize what they learn.

Each lesson section in Group's Active Bible Curriculum plays an important part in active learning:

The **Opener** involves kids in the topic in fun and unusual ways.

The **Action and Reflection** includes an experience designed to evoke specific feelings in the students. This section also processes those feelings through "How did you feel?" questions and applies the message to situations kids face.

The **Bible Application** actively connects the topic with the Bible. It helps kids see how the Bible is relevant to the situations they face.

The **Commitment** helps students internalize the Bible's message and commit to make changes in their lives.

The **Closing** funnels the lesson's message into a time of creative reflection and prayer.

When you put all the sections together, you get a lesson that's fun to teach. And kids get messages they'll remember.

● Read the Introduction, the Course Objectives and This Course at a Glance.

● Decide how you'll publicize the course using the clip art on the Publicity Page (p. 9). Prepare fliers, newsletter articles and posters as needed.

● Look at the Bonus Ideas (p. 43) and decide which ones you'll use.

● Read the opening statements, Objectives and Bible Basis for the lesson. The Bible Basis shows how specific passages relate to junior highers and middle schoolers today.

● Choose which Opener and Closing options to use. Each is appropriate for a different kind of group.

● Gather necessary supplies from This Lesson at a Glance.

● Read each section of the lesson. Adjust where necessary for your class size and meeting room.

● The approximate minutes listed give you an idea of how long each activity will take. Each lesson is designed to take 35 to 60 minutes. Shorten or lengthen activities as needed to fit your group.

● If you see you're going to have extra time, do an activity or two from the "If You Still Have Time . . ." box or from the Bonus Ideas (p. 43).

● Dive into the activities with the kids. Don't be a spectator. The lesson will be more successful and rewarding to both you and your students.

● Though some kids may at first think certain activities are "silly," they'll enjoy them, and they'll remember the messages from these activities long after the lesson is over. As one Active Bible Curriculum™ user has said, "I can ask the kids questions about a lesson I did three weeks ago, and they actually remember what I taught!" And that's the whole idea of teaching . . . isn't it?

Have fun with the activities you lead. Remember, it is Jesus who encourages us to become "like little children." Besides, how often do your kids get *permission* to express their child-like qualities?

● The answers given after discussion questions are responses your students *might* give. They aren't the only answers or the "right" answers. If needed, use them to spark discussion. Kids won't always say what you wish they'd say. That's why some of the responses given are negative or controversial. If someone responds negatively, don't be shocked. Accept the person and use the opportunity to explore other angles of the issue.

THIS COURSE AT A GLANCE

Before you dive into the lessons, familiarize yourself with each lesson aim. Then read the scripture passages.
- Study them as a background to the lessons.
- Use them as a basis for your personal devotions.
- Think about how they relate to kids' circumstances today.

LESSON 1: WHAT IS HEAVEN?

Lesson Aim: To help junior highers understand the biblical descriptions of heaven.

Bible Basis: Romans 8:18-25 and Revelation 21:1-7, 15-27.

LESSON 2: WHAT IS HELL?

Lesson Aim: To help junior highers explore various perspectives on hell.

Bible Basis: Luke 16:19-31; John 3:16-21; and Revelation 20:1-3, 7-10.

LESSON 3: WHO WILL GO TO HEAVEN?

Lesson Aim: To help junior highers understand what it takes to get to heaven.

Bible Basis: Matthew 13:24-30, 36-43; John 3:14-18; and John 14:1-6.

LESSON 4: HEAVEN ON EARTH

Lesson Aim: To help junior highers live like citizens of heaven while they're still on Earth.

Bible Basis: Matthew 6:9-13 and 1 John 3:2-3.

PUBLICITY PAGE

Grab your junior highers' attention! Photocopy this page, and then cut out and paste the clip art of your choice in your church bulletin or newsletter to advertise this course on heaven and hell. Or photocopy and use the ready-made flier as a bulletin insert. Permission to photocopy clip art is granted for local church use.

Splash the clip art on posters, fliers or even postcards! Just add the vital details: the date and time the course begins and where you'll meet.

Heaven & HELL

Heaven & HELL

A 4-week junior high and middle school course on the realities of heaven and hell

Come to _____

On _____

At _____

Come learn what heaven and hell are really like!

WHAT IS HEAVEN?

Real freedom. Total happiness. Unending peace. Are they ever really possible? The Bible's good news: Yes! The bad news: You have to wait until you die.

We all want instant gratification. But part of living the Christian life is learning to lay aside immediate pleasure for a greater fulfillment later. Kids need to see heaven as the place of ultimate fulfillment— a fulfillment that makes even the bad times in our lives now seem insignificant.

LESSON AIM

To help junior highers understand the biblical descriptions of heaven.

OBJECTIVES

Students will:
- consider what heaven might be like or what it might feel like to get a glimpse of heaven;
- explore how to make heaven a personal experience while still living on Earth; and
- experience the difficulty of understanding what heaven is like.

BIBLE BASIS

ROMANS 8:18-25
REVELATION 21:1-7, 15-27

Look up the following scriptures. Then read the background paragraphs to see how the passages relate to your junior highers and middle schoolers.

In **Romans 8:18-25**, believers, and all creation, long for God to bring release from death and decay to a new form of existence. In this passage, Paul talks to the believers in Rome about their release from the bonds of a fallen Earth. He talks about how we wait with excitement to be granted the new life of heaven.

Kids can understand what it means to wait with

excitement. They want more freedom. They want to be treated like adults. They long for release from the bondage of old rules that seem childish to them. But through this passage, kids can learn there is something far more exciting to wait for.

Revelation 21:1-7, 15-27 describes the new heaven and new Earth, including details about the size and construction materials for the New Jerusalem. Because Revelation is apocalyptic literature (revealing hidden things), it is filled with visions, symbols and figurative language. Even so, the book clearly conveys the truth that God is in control of history and that he has definite plans for the end of time. John's glimpse of heaven in this passage can give us all a renewed understanding of our Lord as one who rules the universe.

Teenagers may struggle with some of the language in Revelation, but that shouldn't keep them from understanding the main theme: Heaven is where God dwells and where he will bring his redeemed people for eternity.

THIS LESSON AT A GLANCE

Section	Minutes	What Students Will Do	Supplies
Opener (Option 1)	5 to 10	**Paradise Pictures**—Draw pictures of heaven.	Newsprint, crayons or markers, tape
(Option 2)		**Heavenly Rewrites**—Decide what would happen if someone caught a glimpse of heaven.	Video movie clip, paper, pencils
Action and Reflection	15 to 20	**Beyond the World We Know**—Enclose themselves in a cocoon of newspapers.	Paper, tape, newspapers
Bible Application	10 to 15	**Dream Vacation**—Decide what they'd see on a trip to heaven. _Man 90 min. Dad saw_	"Dream Vacation" handouts (p. 18), Bibles, pencils
Commitment	5 to 10	**Taste and See**—Compare tasting candy to experiencing heaven.	Bag of candy
Closing (Option 1)	up to 5	**One Nation**—Make a flag that represents heaven.	Magazines, scissors, tape, newsprint, marker
(Option 2)		**Top Groaners**—Find ways their hope of heaven can wipe out things that make them groan now.	Newsprint, tape, marker

The Lesson

(handwritten: l.)

☑ OPTION 1: PARADISE PICTURES

(handwritten: Draw pictures of heaven)

Give each person a sheet of newsprint and crayons or markers. Have kids each draw a quick, simple picture that represents how they visualize heaven. Have them each include their own "dwelling place" in heaven and fill it with the things they think might be there. Also have them each draw a stick figure of themselves showing what they think they might be doing in heaven. When everyone's finished, tape the artwork to the walls and gather kids in a circle. After kids briefly explain their pictures, ask:

- **How are the pictures similar to each other? How are they different?**
- **Why does the picture of heaven vary from one person to the next?** (Maybe heaven will be different for each person; nobody knows exactly what it will be like.)
- **How does our society picture heaven?** (An angel strumming a harp on a cloud; a place where there's nothing but pleasure.)
- **Is society's picture of heaven attractive to you? Why or why not?** (No, it sounds boring; yes, because there will be no pain there.)
- **What do you think is wrong with society's picture of heaven?** (It's too boring; it seems stupid.)

Say: **There is much about heaven we won't really know until we get there, but today we're going to see how the Bible describes the place we call heaven.**

☐ OPTION 2: HEAVENLY REWRITES

Have kids watch a video clip of a "crying scene" in a modern or classic movie. Set the scene by explaining why the person is so distraught.

After the clip, form pairs and give each pair a sheet of paper and a pencil. Have them each develop a story line for the action that might follow the crying scene if the crier suddenly caught a glimpse of heaven. When pairs are ready, have volunteers act out their scene completions. Then ask:

- **Why did you finish the scene the way you did?** (We thought the beauty of heaven would stop their crying; we thought the brilliance of heaven would make them bow down.)
- **Is it really possible that someday sorrow and crying could be totally wiped out? Why or why not?** (Sure, if the Bible says so; I'm not sure, I don't see how *all* sorrow could be wiped out.)
- **What's the main thing about heaven that makes you want to go there?** (Jesus is there; there'll be no problems in heaven.)

Say: **The Bible says heaven is a place where God will wipe away every tear from our eyes (Revelation 21:4). Let's look a little deeper into what else the Bible says about what heaven will be like.**

BEYOND THE WORLD WE KNOW

Give kids each a sheet of paper and have them tear the paper to represent something they value in this world. For example, they could make something to represent their car or a friendship. When kids are ready, have them explain what they created.

Form groups of six or fewer, and give each group tape and a stack of newspapers. Say: **Using the newspapers and tape, create a "cocoon" in which your entire group can be completely hidden from my sight. You can use any other props you can find in this room.**

Give kids several minutes to create their cocoons. Make sure kids are completely concealed in their newspaper cocoons, and instruct them to take their torn-paper creations inside with them. When groups are all "cocooned," ask:

● **How does it feel to be sealed off from the rest of the room?** (It's fun to hide; it feels a little stuffy.)

● **What do you think I'm doing?**

Say: **Let's say your little cocoon is like life on Earth. You have all your friends here, and all the things you value. But there's a whole lot more in this room than what you can see.**

Ask:

● **How is this like the difference between Earth and heaven?** (We can only see and understand a little of the whole picture while we're alive on Earth; in heaven, we'll understand everything about life.)

● **From this experience, why is it hard for us to understand what life in heaven must be like?** (We can only see our limited experiences; heaven could be totally different from life on Earth, and we can't see it to know what it's like.)

● **How does this experience make you feel about heaven? Explain.** (Curious, because I wonder how it will be different from life on Earth; excited, because I want to see what it's like where God lives.)

Say: **It really is hard to understand what heaven is like. Our limited human language falls short because we don't have the words to describe heaven. Fortunately, God has not left us completely in the dark. We have his Word to help us understand the reality of heaven, even though it's totally different from life here on Earth.**

DREAM VACATION

2.

Have group members tear their way out of their cocoons, and give each person a photocopy of the "Dream Vacation" handout (p. 18), a Bible and a pencil. Have someone read aloud Revelation 21:1-7, 15-27. Then say: **Suppose you were given a chance to check out heaven before you die. What would you like to see on this unusual vacation?**

Have kids complete their handouts by following the instructions written there. When kids are finished, have them form groups of four, and take turns telling their group members what their favorite attraction is and why.

When groups are finished, have kids read Romans 8:18-25. Have kids write on the back of their handouts three ways their knowledge of heaven can affect the way they live their lives now. When kids are ready, have them tell what they wrote. Then say: **Heaven may sound too good to be true, but it's a reality God expects us to take seriously. And just as you've pointed out through your responses, the reality of heaven should affect the way we live today.**

TASTE AND SEE   *3.*

Tell kids you have a bag of treats you want to share with them. Without actually saying the food is candy, describe it in as many ways as you can, including color, taste, shape, texture and smell. After you've described it, ask:

● **Do you feel I've shared the treats with you? Why or why not?** (No, I haven't tasted anything; no, I haven't even seen them yet; yes, you told us about them.)

● **How is my describing the treats like all the talking we've done today about heaven?** (Our descriptions all fall short of the experience of heaven; talking about it and experiencing it are two different things.)

Have kids close their eyes and open their mouths. One by one, place a treat in each person's mouth. As kids enjoy the sudden burst of flavor, ask:

● **How did it feel to finally get to taste the candy? Explain.** (It was good to finally experience what you described; great, because I was afraid it wouldn't be what you described.)

● **How is finally tasting the candy like it will be to experience heaven?** (It becomes a personal experience; we'll live it instead of just talking about it.)

Have kids form a circle. Then ask:

● **How can we make heaven a personal experience while we still live here on Earth?** (We can live with the expectation of being there someday; we can learn more about it.)

Say: **If we try, we can see little glimpses of heaven all around us, both in the people of God and in God's creation.**

Go around the circle and have kids each complete this statement about the person to their right: "One way I see a little bit of heaven in you is . . . "

didya Trust me
" really know what I was
giving

Told you about treat
didn't totally know
like until you
heaven tasted

Was it good?

Table Talk

The Table Talk activity in this course helps junior highers and middle schoolers talk with their parents about heaven and hell.

If you choose to use the Table Talk activity, this is a good time to show students the "Table Talk" handout (p. 19). Ask them to spend time with their parents completing it.

Before kids leave, give them each a photocopy of the "Table Talk" handout to take home, or tell them you'll be sending it to their parents. Tell kids to be prepared to report on their experience with the handout next week.

Or use the Table Talk idea found in the Bonus Ideas (p. 44) for a meeting based on the handout.

CLOSING
(up to 5 minutes)

put
images on flag
that represent
glimpses
of
heaven
light
gold street
feast
food
table
smile
fountain of water
Tree of life

☐ OPTION 1: ONE NATION

Give kids each a magazine and scissors. Tell kids to look through the magazines to find images of things or people that give them "glimpses" of heaven. While kids are looking through the magazines, tape a sheet of newsprint to the wall and draw a large flag shape on it.

When kids are finished, have them tape their images on the flag shape. Once the "flag of heaven" is complete, have volunteers explain their images.

Close with prayer. Thank God for a place like heaven and ask him to help your kids keep the excitement of heaven in mind as they live their lives. *this week*

☐ OPTION 2: TOP GROANERS

Tape a sheet of newsprint to the wall, and ask kids to brainstorm things that make them "groan" in life. List at least five items. When the list is done, form groups of no more than five, rip apart the five items and distribute the items among the groups. It's okay if groups have more than one item.

When all the groups are in place, have group members brainstorm ways they can bring a little of the excitement of heaven into their "groaner" situations. After a few minutes, call time and have volunteers report what they brainstormed.

Have kids form a circle. Then say: **Even in the worst situation, we can remember the greatness of heaven to make that situation better.**

Close with prayer, thanking God for a place like heaven and asking him to help your kids keep the excitement of heaven in mind as they live their lives.

If You Still Have Time . . .

Respond to the Critic—Have kids respond to this statement made by an imaginary critic: "All this talk of heaven is just a crutch for weak people who can't stand to live without a future pie-in-the-sky fantasy. Get real! Stop living in a fantasy world! Nobody can prove heaven exists, so start living now. That's all there is!"

He's Here, Too—Tell kids the main reason heaven will be so wonderful is Jesus is there. Ask kids what their first conversation with Jesus in heaven might be like. What would they ask him? Say: Being in heaven with Jesus will be awesome, but it's important to remember we have Jesus' Spirit living within us right now. We don't have to wait for heaven to have a close relationship with him.

5. Make Jesus part of your life
Best Friend / don't ignore him
Keep friendship alive

praye   This week home + school

DREAM VACATION!

Revelation 21:1-7, 15-27

Look at the "attractions" below, and read the verses from Revelation where they're spoken of. Then pick the top three attractions you'd want to visit on a vacation to heaven, and rank them in order of importance to you. Be ready to tell which attraction is your favorite and why you picked it.

Visit the New Jerusalem! Imagine these awesome attractions . . .

___ Set Sail on the Sea That Disappeared! (21:1-5)

___ Drink From the Spring of the Water of Life! (21:6-7)

___ Touch the Foundation of Precious Stones! (21:15-20)

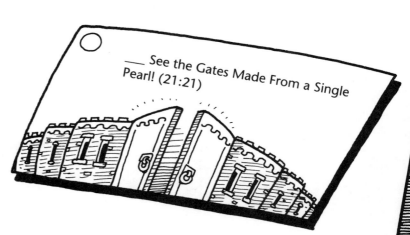

___ See the Gates Made From a Single Pearl! (21:21)

___ Walk the Streets of Gold! (21:21)

___ Meet God Almighty! (21:22)

___ Experience the Land of No Night! (21:23-27)

Table Talk

To the Parent: We're involved in a junior high course at church called *Heaven & Hell*. We'd like you and your son or daughter to spend some time discussing this important topic. Use this "Table Talk" handout to help you.

Parent

Do some preliminary research in the Bible on the topic of heaven and hell, perhaps using a concordance. When you meet with your junior higher, complete the following sentences:

- When I heard the words "heaven" and "hell" as a teenager, I usually felt...
- One thing about heaven that makes me look forward to it is...
- One thing about the idea of hell that bothers me is...
- My basic beliefs about heaven and hell right now could be summarized as...

Junior higher

Complete these statements:

- To me, life after death seems...
- One joyful thought I have about heaven is...
- One fear I have related to heaven and hell is...
- What I'd really like to know more about this topic is...

Parent and junior higher

Read through Luke 16:19-26 and Revelation 21 together and then complete these statements:

- Heaven will be exciting because...
- What the Bible says about heaven helps me...
- What the Bible says about hell helps me...
- Usually we don't talk much about death and eternity because...
- It sometimes seems tough to live as a "citizen of heaven" at home because...
- For me to live more heavenly minded, I would have to...
- One way our family could become more heavenly minded would be...

LESSON 2

WHAT IS HELL?

C. S. Lewis said, "I would pay any price to be able to say truthfully 'All will be saved.' " But he concluded he couldn't. We'd rather not admit it, but it is possible to lose in life, to spend eternity regretting one's utter self-centeredness. We can't be exactly sure what hell is, but we certainly can't ignore it—Jesus spoke more often of hell than he did of heaven.

Kids need to grapple with what hell is and develop a biblical concept of it. This lesson helps kids do just that.

LESSON AIM

To help junior highers explore various perspectives on hell.

OBJECTIVES

Students will:
● examine their feelings about the idea of punishment for wrongdoing;
● examine Bible characters who didn't make it to heaven;
● consider the Bible's descriptions of hell; and
● commit to follow Christ.

BIBLE BASIS

LUKE 16:19-31
JOHN 3:16-21
REVELATION 20:1-3, 7-10

Look up the following scriptures. Then read the background paragraphs to see how the passages relate to your junior highers and middle schoolers.

Luke 16:19-31 relates Christ's parable describing the eternal fates of a selfish man and a beggar.

The Pharisees had criticized Jesus for associating with sinners. In response, Jesus told them this parable. It points out the distinction between the values of earthly life and heaven. Kids primarily live in the "now." Through this parable, Jesus calls us to look at what we're building for our future "now."

John 3:16-21 summarizes the essence of God's plan and the common human response to it.

Jesus' statements in this passage are part of his response to Nicodemus, who wanted to know how a person could be "born again." Jesus explained that eternal life could come only through his own death, and it could be gained only through faith in him.

Kids may think it's not fair that some people go to hell. But Jesus points out in this passage that his purpose in coming to Earth was to bring eternal life to all who believe in him. By rejecting him, people are rejecting the eternal life he offers.

Revelation 20:1-3, 7-10 describes Satan's ultimate doom. Hell, whatever it is, was intended for the devil and his angels. But people's rejection of God has opened the way for their spirits to be condemned to hell along with Satan and his kind.

THIS LESSON AT A GLANCE

Section	Minutes	What Students Will Do	Supplies
Opener (Option 1)	5 to 10	**Soundtracks From Hell**—Develop an album cover for a record about hell.	Paper, markers, tape
(Option 2)		**Bogus Journey?**—Watch a video clip of hell from *Bill and Ted's Bogus Journey*.	Video movie clip
Action and Reflection	10 to 15	**Choose Your Punishment**—Send each other to No-Cookie Hell.	"The Punishments" box (p. 23), scissors (or 3×5 cards, pen), tape
Bible Application	10 to 15	**Three Who Don't Make It**—Examine Bible characters who didn't make it to heaven.	"Three Who Don't Make It" handouts (p. 27), pencils, Bibles
Commitment	10 to 15	**Hell-Views Lineup**—Explore different views of the nature of hell.	Bibles, tape, newsprint, marker
Closing (Option 1)	up to 5	**Measuring Eternity**—Imagine what eternity is like.	
(Option 2)		**Greatest Sinners**—List the world's greatest sinners.	Paper, pencils

The Lesson

☐ OPTION 1: SOUNDTRACKS FROM HELL

Tell kids you're going to have a contest to see who can develop the best album cover for a new record called *Gone to Hell!* Give kids each a sheet of paper and markers, and let

OPENER
(5 to 10 minutes)

kids work on their creative renderings for a few minutes. When the album covers are complete, let kids vote on the following categories: Most Gruesome, Most Fantastic and Most Like Hell Really Is. Pick one piece of artwork for each category as "winners" and display them on the wall. Ask:

● **Was it hard to think of a "hellish" cover for this album? Why or why not?** (No, everybody knows what hell is like; yes, I didn't like to think about the gross images.)

● **Why do you think most people consider hell a gruesome and painful place?** (The Bible says so; they relate it to horror movies.)

● **How does it feel to think that hell is a real place?** (It's a little frightening; I want to know where it is.)

Say: **To help us think about what hell might be like, let's visit a special kind of hell: No-Cookie Hell!**

☐ OPTION 2: BOGUS JOURNEY?

Note: This option involves showing a brief clip from the video *Bill and Ted's Bogus Journey*. The clip may contain profanity, but it shows a typical attempt at making hell humorous and could be an effective discussion-starter for this class. Preview the video to locate a short clip that's appropriate for your use.

Start your class by showing the two- to three-minute scene from *Bill and Ted's Bogus Journey* where they first descend into hell. After the clip, ask:

● **How did you feel as you viewed this scene?** (It was funny; I wondered where they got their information about hell.)

● **In your opinion, how accurate is this portrayal of hell? Explain.** (Not at all, since there's no fire; it doesn't seem harsh enough.)

● **What would you change to make Bill and Ted's hell more like the "real item" you have in mind?** (Make it all a pool of fire; separate Bill and Ted and add more physical pain.)

Say: **Most everyone has ideas about what hell is like, even Bill and Ted! But how do we know we're right? To help us think about what hell might be like, let's visit a special kind of hell: No-Cookie Hell!**

Table Talk Follow-Up

If you sent the "Table Talk" handout (p. 19) to parents last week, discuss students' reactions to the activity. Ask volunteers to share what they learned from the discussion with their parents.

CHOOSE YOUR PUNISHMENT

Say: **Hell isn't a subject to be taken lightly. But to help us understand the implications of hell, we're going to look at a fictional situation.**

Photocopy and cut apart the punishments listed in "The Punishments" box in the margin. Or, write them each on a separate 3×5 card.

Have kids form a circle and then read aloud this scenario: **You were warned repeatedly that you could *not* have another cookie. But in a moment of extreme temptation, you slipped into the kitchen, reached into the cookie jar and pulled out two chocolate chip cookies.**

You thought about putting them back, but then you heard someone coming, so you stuffed the cookies into your mouth and headed for the back door. Suddenly, a booming voice said: "I saw that! I am the Cookie King. Choose your punishment!" After the Cookie King gives you your choices, you must choose which punishment the person to your right must suffer.

Pick six people to hold the slips of paper listing the punishments (or the 3×5 cards). Challenge your class to rank the punishments from "worst" to "least bad."

Allow kids several minutes to discuss how the punishments should be ranked. Once the order is decided, tape the slips (or cards) to the wall from worst (on the left) to least bad (on the right). Then have kids each choose the punishment for the person on their right. Once everyone has been assigned a punishment, have kids stand in front of the appropriate punishment. Ask:

● **How do you feel about your punishment? Explain.** (Awful, it seems too severe; okay, it's not one of the worst punishments.)

● **How did you feel about assigning a punishment? Explain.** (Okay until I saw that other people got easier punishments; bad, I didn't want to make the person mad at me.)

● **Is this the way hell is? Why or why not?** (No, because the punishment is the same for everyone; yes, because we all get punished for what we do.)

● **Do you think it's fair for some people to go to hell and others to go to heaven? Why or why not?** (Yes, because they made the choices that led them there; no, everyone should be treated the same.)

● **Does God arbitrarily assign a punishment for each person on Earth, just as we did in this activity? Why or why not?** (No, God treats each person according to what he or she deserves; no, people condemn themselves by their actions; yes, it's all a matter of luck who gets into heaven.)

Say: **No-Cookie Hell may not be much like the real hell, but it gives us a chance to feel what it might be like to be condemned because of our actions—even actions we may**

ACTION AND REFLECTION
(10 to 15 minutes)

The Punishments

● Go to No-Cookie Hell: Be separated from cookies forever.

● Have your taste buds surgically removed.

● Eat six cookies—and drink a quart of milk that's been sitting in the sun for two weeks.

● Bake in the cookie oven until you're light and crispy.

● Have flour sprinkled on your eyeballs.

● Go to school with a stick of butter in each shoe.

think are okay. Now let's take a look at what the Bible says about the real hell and who goes there.

THREE WHO DON'T MAKE IT

Give kids each a photocopy of the "Three Who Don't Make It" handout (p. 27) and a pencil. Form three groups, assign each group one section of the handout and give each group a Bible. Have groups read through the passages and work together to complete their sections of the handout.

When groups are finished, have them tell what they wrote. After all the groups have shared, ask:

● **What do these three situations tell you about hell?** (It's hot; it's a place of condemnation.)

● **What do these three situations tell you about who goes to hell?** (Selfish people; Satan; those who don't believe in Jesus.)

● **Based on these passages, do you think God *sends* people to hell? Why or why not?** (Yes, if they deserve it; no, people condemn themselves by their own choices.)

Say: **It's not clear exactly what hell is like. But it's certainly not a place we want to live. Let's look a little deeper into how we can avoid this "worst of all places."**

HELL-VIEWS LINEUP   *7 scriptures*

Form pairs and give each pair a Bible. Assign each pair one of these passages: Matthew 8:12; Mark 9:47-48; Luke 13:27-28; Philippians 3:18-19; 2 Thessalonians 1:8-9; Jude 7; and Revelation 21:8. It's okay if multiple pairs have the same passage. Have pairs read their passages and come up with short phrases to describe hell based on the passages. While kids are working, tape a sheet of newsprint to the wall. When pairs are ready, have them each write their phrase on the newsprint.

When all the phrases are written, say: **The Bible doesn't always call hell a place of fire. Even with the Bible passages, people still disagree about the nature of hell and its purpose.**

Briefly share with kids the quick descriptions of the four major interpretations of hell in which people believe (see the box in the margin). Have kids each choose the view they like best and tell what they chose.

This might be a good time to express your church's beliefs about hell. You might even want to have your pastor visit your class.

Ask:

● **What are some things we can know for sure about hell?** (I don't want to go there; it's not a good place.)

● **What can we do to help us avoid hell?** (Commit to live for God; choose to follow Jesus.)

BIBLE APPLICATION
(10 to 15 minutes)

COMMITMENT
(10 to 15 minutes)

punishment   pain
separation   fire
from God   isolation
forever   eternal)

Views of Hell

1. **See You There!:** Eventually, God will save everyone, so hell is a temporary place.

2. **Loss of Fellowship:** Hell is the Bible's way of describing complete separation from God's presence and possibly total isolation from any other being.

3. **Annihilation Sensation:** There's really no lasting torment because wicked souls are simply destroyed at death.

4. **Eternal Flame:** It's real fire, with real physical pain forever.

Say: **Let's join hands and pray, committing ourselves to live for Christ in this life.**

Have kids join hands and pray together. After the prayer, have kids tell the person across from them one reason they're glad that person has committed to follow Christ. Make sure no one is missed.

OPTION 1: MEASURING ETERNITY

Say: **Let's close today by trying to imagine what eternity might be like—for those in heaven and in hell.**

Have kids close their eyes and remain perfectly silent for three minutes. Tell kids their task is to gauge the passage of time and raise their hands when they think exactly three minutes have passed. After they're all done, have kids give a standing ovation to the person who comes closest to the three-minute mark.

Say: **When doing something that isn't very fun or interesting, even three minutes can seem like an eternity. People in heaven will spend eternity with God, which will never be boring. But "eternity" is also the word the Bible sometimes uses to describe the fate of those destined for hell. If our three-minute test is even a faint parallel of hell, it's a place we all sure want to avoid.**

Close with prayer, thanking God for showing kids the way to heaven and the way to avoid hell.

OPTION 2: GREATEST SINNERS

Form groups of three and give each group a sheet of paper and a pencil. Have groups each create a list of the greatest sinners in history. After a few minutes, have groups tell what they wrote. Then ask:

● **Do these people deserve to go to hell? Why or why not?** (Yes, they are terrible people; yes, they chose not to follow God; no, God should forgive them.)

● **Do you deserve to go to hell? Why or why not?** (No, because I trust Jesus; yes, I sin just like those bad people do.)

Say: **The Bible says whoever sins deserves to go to hell. But when we become Christians, we're freed from the punishment for our sins. Let's close today by thanking God for making a way for us to avoid eternal punishment.**

Close with prayer, thanking God for sending his son to die for us that we might be able to gain eternal life.

CLOSING
(up to 5 minutes)

If You Still Have Time . . .

Staying Out of Hell—Tape a sheet of newsprint on a wall and have kids brainstorm ways to talk to their friends about accepting Jesus' gift of eternal life and avoiding hell. Have kids each choose one approach to use with a non-Christian friend during the coming week.

My Personal Hell—Have kids tell what they think is the worst personal hell and explain why. Read aloud 1 John 1:9 and remind kids they don't have to be afraid of hell because of Jesus' love and forgiveness for each of them.

THREE WHO DON'T MAKE IT

Have someone in your group read aloud the passage assigned to your group. Then answer the questions in the appropriate section of the handout.

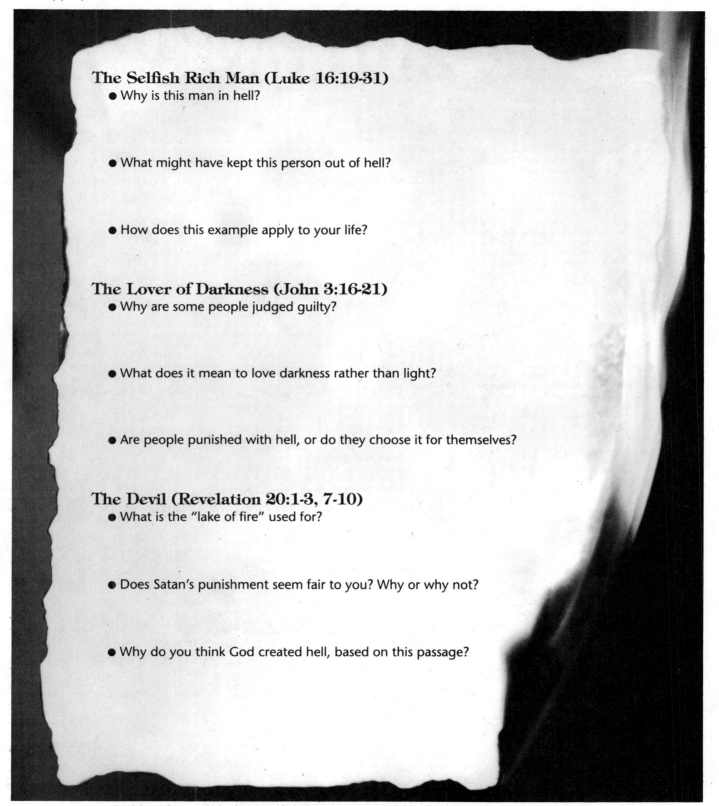

The Selfish Rich Man (Luke 16:19-31)
- Why is this man in hell?

- What might have kept this person out of hell?

- How does this example apply to your life?

The Lover of Darkness (John 3:16-21)
- Why are some people judged guilty?

- What does it mean to love darkness rather than light?

- Are people punished with hell, or do they choose it for themselves?

The Devil (Revelation 20:1-3, 7-10)
- What is the "lake of fire" used for?

- Does Satan's punishment seem fair to you? Why or why not?

- Why do you think God created hell, based on this passage?

1 John 1:9   remind don't have to be afraid
if they choose + accept Jesus

LESSON 3

WHO WILL GO TO HEAVEN?

As with many Bible doctrines, the teachings about heaven give great truths but leave certain questions at least partly unanswered. Ultimately, it's God who decides who will make it to heaven. But through Christ he has provided the only way we can have that eternal life with him. This lesson helps kids sort out what some people and the Bible say about who goes to heaven.

LESSON AIM

To help junior highers understand what it takes to get to heaven.

OBJECTIVES

Students will:
● explore who might go to heaven;
● question whether God is fair; and
● commit to live for Jesus on Earth.

BIBLE BASIS
MATTHEW 13:24-30; 36-43
JOHN 3:14-18
JOHN 14:1-6

Look up the following scriptures. Then read the background paragraphs to see how the passages relate to your junior highers and middle schoolers.

In **Matthew 13:24-30, 36-43**, Jesus tells a parable about weeds and wheat and explains its meaning.

Jesus told this parable while speaking to a large crowd that wanted to know about the nature of the kingdom of God. Through this parable we discover how God will choose which people will enter heaven.

Kids understand what it means to compare themselves to others. But in this parable, Jesus makes it clear that only God can tell who will go to heaven.

In **John 3:14-18**, we find Jesus' purpose in coming to

Earth— to bring us the possibility of eternal life.

This passage clearly states that belief in Jesus brings eternal life. Whatever other people say about how to get to heaven, we have a clear statement from Jesus himself.

Kids will likely be familiar with John 3:16— maybe too familiar. But the truth is still the same. Having faith in Jesus and what he did for us on the cross is the only way we know of to gain entrance to eternal life with God in heaven.

In **John 14:1-6**, Jesus tells his disciples about the heavenly home he's preparing for them.

Jesus wanted to help his disciples cope with his coming betrayal and crucifixion. He gave them hope by telling them he was leaving to prepare a place for them, so they could come join him.

Teenagers, too, can find comfort in knowing Jesus is preparing a place for them in heaven. With heaven as their ultimate home, kids can learn how to live life on Earth as "travelers" rather than "residents."

THIS LESSON AT A GLANCE

Section	Minutes	What Students Will Do	Supplies
Opener (Option 1)	5 to 10	**The Whole Picture**—Put together a puzzle that's missing a piece.	40- to 50-piece puzzle
(Option 2)		**The Law**—Create laws by which all people should live.	Chalkboard or newsprint, chalk or markers
Action and Reflection	10 to 15	**Choice Chairs**—Go to "hell" based on which chair they sit in.	Masking tape, paper, marker, snacks
Bible Application	15 to 20	**Wheat or Weed?**—Decide who will make it to heaven.	"Wheat or Weed?" handouts (p. 34), pencils, Bibles
Commitment	5 to 10	**Key Reminders**—Discuss the "keys" they have to open the door of heaven.	Blank keys, Bible, fine-point markers
Closing (Option 1)	up to 5	**Light of Heaven**—Light candles to illustrate how they can help others see the way to heaven.	Candles, matches
(Option 2)		**A Place of Perfection**—Find scenes that make them think of heaven.	Travel magazines

The Lesson

☐ OPTION 1: THE WHOLE PICTURE

Before class, remove one puzzle piece from a 40- to 50-piece puzzle. Keep this piece where kids won't see it.

Without letting kids know there's a piece missing, dump the pieces of the puzzle in a pile in the center of the room. Tell kids to complete the puzzle. If you have more than 10 people in your class, form groups of no more than 10 and give each group a different puzzle with one piece missing.

Allow kids to work until they realize they don't have all the pieces to finish the puzzle. Hold up the missing piece and ask:

● **How did you feel when you realized you didn't have all the pieces?** (Frustrated; confused.)

● **What other experiences have you had where you didn't have the "whole picture"?**

● **How does this activity relate to the question of who will make it to heaven?** (Not everyone will because they don't have the whole picture of Christ's death and resurrection; some people strive to make it on their own, but God alone has the "missing piece.")

Say: **According to the Bible, some people will go to heaven and some will not. Although the Bible doesn't tell everything about who will go to heaven and who won't, it does give us all the information we need to choose for ourselves where we'll go. Today, we're going to talk about who will make it to heaven.**

☐ OPTION 2: THE LAW

On a chalkboard or sheet of newsprint, draw a large outline of Moses' stone tablets. Give kids each a piece of chalk or a marker, and tell kids they've been transported back to a time when absolutely no laws existed. Tell kids it's their job to create all the laws— no matter how minor— that humans should know and observe. If you have more than 12 kids, you might want to form multiple groups and have a separate set of "stone tablets" for each group.

As kids write, encourage them to think of "personal" laws they live by as well as more "general" laws that apply to everyone.

When kids are finished, ask:

● **What would the world be like without laws?** (Chaotic; violent.)

● **How did laws first come into being?** (God brought them; people set down rules so they could live together in peace.)

● **Do you automatically know what's morally right or wrong? Why or why not?** (Yes, because God tells us; no, I think it depends on our environment.)

● **What do you think determines who will go to heaven?** (God does, based on what kind of people we've been in this life; it depends on a person's faith.)

Say: **Many people think "good" people go to heaven and "bad" people go to hell. But that's not necessarily true. Today, we're going to talk about who will make it to heaven.**

CHOICE CHAIRS

Before class, put a small piece of masking tape out of sight on the bottom of about one-third of the chairs. Write "Heaven" on one sheet of paper and "Hell" on another. Tape these signs on opposite ends of the room.

When it's time for this activity, have kids form a circle with their chairs. Under the "Heaven" sign, place snacks kids will enjoy.

Have kids each look under their chair and remove the tape if it's there.

Say: **Those of you who have a piece of tape get to go to heaven. Please take your chair and move over next to the sign marked "Heaven." Enjoy the snacks. Those of you who have no tape must go to hell. Please stand next to the sign marked "Hell."**

When kids are in place, ask:

● **How do you feel being where you are? Explain.** (Great, I made it to heaven; angry, because this wasn't a fair way to make this decision.)

● **How is this activity similar to the way we end up in either heaven or hell?** (It isn't, because it was just a random choice; we don't actually decide where we go.)

● **How is this activity different?** (We had no choice in this activity; whether we go to heaven is based on our faith, not on a random choice.)

● **If the pieces of tape represented making a faith commitment to Jesus, how would that change your view of this activity?** (Then it makes sense, since those who have faith in Jesus go to heaven; it still isn't right, since those with the tape were just lucky.)

Say: **God does ultimately decide who will enter his heaven, but he has provided all the information we need to get there.**

Have your kids in "heaven" share the snacks with the rest of the class.

ACTION AND REFLECTION
(10 to 15 minutes)

BIBLE APPLICATION
(15 to 20 minutes)

WHEAT OR WEED?

Form four groups and give each group a photocopy of the "Wheat or Weed?" handout (p. 34), a pencil and a Bible. Assign each group one section of the handout.

Have groups each read Matthew 13:24-30, 36-43 and John 3:14-18, and then complete their section of the handout based on the information in the passages.

When groups are finished, have them explain their answers and ask other kids whether or not they agree. Allow several minutes for open discussion. Then ask:

● **Does the Bible give easy answers about who will go to heaven? Why or why not?** (No, it doesn't talk about other religions much; yes, it's clear only people who believe in Jesus will get to heaven.)

● **Why do you think we don't have easy answers to these situations?** (God is in control and he just lets us know what we need to know; we don't know the whole situation.)

● **How does the "gray area" concerning who will go to heaven affect the way you live your life?** (I want to be sure I'm going, so I'll stay away from things I'm not sure about; I want to help people who are living in the gray areas.)

● **Based on what we've read so far in the Bible, who will go to heaven?** (Those who believe in Jesus and follow him; those who turn away from doing bad things and live for God.)

Say: **Rather than worrying about what we don't know, we need to make sure we aren't ignoring what we do know about going to heaven. Through Jesus and the Word, God has shown us all we need to know to get to heaven. But we must decide to listen and live by what he has said.**

COMMITMENT
(5 to 10 minutes)

KEY REMINDERS

Give each kid a blank key. (You can purchase these cheaply at most drugstores or hardware stores.) Read aloud John 14:1-6. Then say: **When Jesus left Earth, he said he was going to prepare a place for each of us, so one day we could join him in heaven. Today I've given you the "key" to opening the door to your mansion in heaven.**

Ask:

● **How can we make sure our key fits the door that leads to heaven?** (By studying the Bible to see what God requires of us; by following Jesus in everything we do.)

Give kids each a fine-point permanent marker and say: **As a sign of our commitment to live for Jesus here on Earth, write "4 J.C." on one side of your key. On the other side, write your own initials.**

Before moving on to the closing, have kids form pairs. Instruct kids each to tell their partner one way they see that person living for Jesus.

☐ OPTION 1: LIGHT OF HEAVEN

Give kids each an unlit candle, and then make your room dark. After kids adjust to the darkness, have them focus on the darkest spot in the room. Light kids' candles, one by one, until all the darkness is overcome.

Say: **Jesus is the true light that shines in darkness. But his disciples are also lights in this world to bring others out of darkness. As we close today, let's remember that as Jesus' disciples we can shine our light and help others discover how they can get to heaven—through faith in Jesus Christ.**

Close with prayer.

☐ OPTION 2: A PLACE OF PERFECTION

Give kids each a travel magazine. Tell kids to tear out scenes that come closest to what they think heaven might look like. After kids explain their choices to the group, ask:

● **Have you ever felt you got a "preview" of heaven? Explain.**

● **Where on Earth do you think we come the closest to seeing glimpses of heaven?** (In the mountains; on the shore.)

Say: **Although the Earth is beautiful, heaven will certainly be much more magnificent. As we close today, let's remember what we have to look forward to.**

Close with prayer, thanking God that through Jesus he's given us a way to get to heaven.

CLOSING
(up to 5 minutes)

If You Still Have Time . . .

Answers to Come—Have kids close their eyes and picture one person they know who they hope to see in heaven. Ask:

● What's the first thing you'll ask this person when you get to heaven?

● What do you think this person will ask you?

An Important Question—Have kids each answer the question, "If you were to die tonight and stand before God, and God asked you, 'Why should I let you in to my heaven?' what would you say?"

Ask kids whether they think the question is fair or appropriate to ask others, and discuss what the question makes people think about.

You may also want to go over again how we get to heaven if kids have trouble answering the question.

WHEAT or WEED?

In your group, read Matthew 13:24-30, 36-43 and John 3:14-18. Then read your assigned situation below and decide, based on the passages, if it would be easy, difficult or impossible for you to determine whether that person will go to heaven. Then talk about why you chose what you did for each situation.

Lakshmi is a Hindu teenager living in India. She worships three gods: Brahma, Siva and Vishnu. She has been taught that her gods are manifestations of the one "all-pervading substance" of the universe (Brahman), which is like a god but is impersonal. She believes she is destined to live life on Earth many times before she becomes pure enough to be reunited with Brahman. Will Lakshmi go to heaven?

Easy   Difficult   Impossible

Bill wandered into a revival meeting held in his hometown one night. At the end of the meeting, he prayed a prayer something like this: "I believe in Jesus as my personal savior." As he looks back on the experience with a grin, he wonders what ever got him to pray something like that. All that wimpy stuff is behind him now. Will Bill go to heaven?

Easy   Difficult   Impossible

Jill is always in church! She is president of her youth group and serves on five different committees. Jill takes pride in being thought of as someone who walks close to God. In fact, she once confided in a friend that she thought God was pretty lucky to have her. Will Jill go to heaven?

Easy   Difficult   Impossible

Professor Bultwynn teaches classes in theology at the big seminary downtown. He knows just about everything that could be known about Christianity and deep theological issues. That's why it surprises some of his students when they see the big mural on his office wall that says, "The most profound truth ever spoken is 'JESUS LOVES ME, THIS I KNOW—FOR THE BIBLE TELLS ME SO.' " Will Professor Bultwynn go to heaven?

Easy   Difficult   Impossible

HEAVEN ON EARTH

Getting to heaven is certainly a worthy goal. But the Bible clearly calls us to be citizens of heaven right now. The choices kids face every day allow them the alternative of responding out of heavenly values or pure self-interest.

Use this session to help kids see how they can help bring a bit of God's kingdom to Earth right now.

To help junior highers live like citizens of heaven while they're still on Earth.

LESSON AIM

Students will:
- **realize how our actions now can affect the future;**
- **consider what it means to be a Christian in a non-Christian world;**
- **explore biblical teachings on Christians as citizens of heaven; and**
- **commit to living on Earth as citizens of heaven.**

OBJECTIVES

Look up the following scriptures. Then read the background paragraphs to see how the passages relate to your junior highers and middle schoolers.

Matthew 6:9-13 is the prayer Jesus taught his disciples.

"The model prayer" was given to the disciples when they asked Jesus to teach them to pray. The prayer includes a startling statement in verse 10: "Your kingdom come, your will be done on earth as it is in heaven." From this one line, it appears heaven and Earth are not totally separate.

Through Jesus' words, kids can understand that Christians' actions on Earth have a direct impact in heaven, since Christians are citizens of heaven through Christ. Kids can

BIBLE BASIS
MATTHEW 6:9-13
1 JOHN 3:2-3

believe the truth that their lives do count for something— both in heaven and on Earth.

In **1 John 3:2-3**, the Apostle John tells us we will eventually be like Christ.

We are going to be just like Jesus someday! The transformation process has already started and will be completed the day we meet Jesus in heaven.

Christian kids are developing characteristics of Jesus in their lives that will finally be complete when they see Jesus face to face. Understanding this process can encourage them to strive to be more like Jesus today.

THIS LESSON AT A GLANCE

Section	Minutes	What Students Will Do	Supplies
Opener (Option 1)	5 to 10	**Preparation Clues**—Guess an activity based on its supplies and preparations list.	3×5 cards, pen, paper, pencils, gum
(Option 2)		**Gift in a Plain Wrapper**—Hold a contest to see who can create the most attractive gift.	Newspaper, toilet paper, brown paper bags, scissors, tape, boxes, bag of candy, rocks
Action and Reflection	10 to 15	**Alien Detection**—Discover who among them are aliens.	Costume supplies
Bible Application	10 to 15	**On Earth as in Heaven**—Discover ways to accomplish God's will in daily life.	Bibles, newsprint, marker, tape, paper, pencil
Commitment	10 to 15	**Paradise Passports**—Create passports to enter heaven.	"Passport to Heaven" handouts (p. 41), pencils, Bibles
Closing (Option 1)	up to 5	**Good Infection**—Describe ways Christianity "infects" people.	Newsprint, tape, marker
(Option 2)		**Joined Together**—Ask God to help them live as heaven's citizens.	Construction paper, marker

The Lesson

OPENER
(5 to 10 minutes)

☐ OPTION 1: PREPARATION CLUES

Before class, write the tasks from the box on page 37 each on a separate 3×5 card.

Form three groups and give each group one of the cards you've prepared.

Tell groups their cards contain tasks they must prepare for. Give groups each a sheet of paper and a pencil, and have them each create a list of supplies and preparations they would need to accomplish this task. Have groups keep their tasks secret.

Once the lists are complete, read them to the class one at a time. Have volunteers guess the activities the other groups were preparing for, based on the supplies and preparations lists. Give a stick of gum to kids who guess correctly.

Ask:

● **How did it feel to try to guess the activities based on the supplies and preparations?** (Really hard; it was fun.)

● **How do people's actions help determine what they'll be doing in the future?** (You can see they're preparing for something; you can predict what might happen to someone based on how they live now.)

● **How is preparing for a task like what a Christian does before going to heaven?** (We live preparing ourselves for eternity in heaven; we try to do what will please God.)

Say: **As Christians, we're all on our way to heaven. But our lifestyles now should make it clear we're living in preparation to go there. Today we'll talk about how we can live as citizens of heaven—on Earth.**

☐ OPTION 2: GIFT IN A PLAIN WRAPPER

Form teams of three and set out several "cheap" wrapping materials— newspaper, toilet paper, brown paper bags, scissors and tape. Tell kids you're going to hold a contest to see which team can create the most attractive gift from the materials provided.

Give teams each a small box where you've placed an object. In one box, place a bag of candy. In all the other boxes, place a small rock. Tape the boxes shut so kids can't look inside. Have kids do their best to create attractive gifts.

After all the gifts are wrapped, have kids vote on which gift is the most beautifully wrapped. Applaud the winners, and then have teams each open their gift and look inside.

When the rocks and the candy have been discovered, ask:

● **How did you feel as you wrapped your box? Explain.** (Frustrated, there weren't a lot of supplies; anxious, because we wanted to win.)

● **How did you feel as you looked inside your box?** (Disappointed; stupid; excited that it was candy.)

● **How is the way people worked on the wrapping like the way people act in real life?** (People spend all their time working on the outside without thinking about what they're

The Tasks

● Walk through a dense jungle to deliver 12 cream pies to a remote village, without being bitten by any insects and without sweating at all.

● Climb the outside of a skyscraper while providing child care for a 2-month-old baby who needs to be fed and changed.

● Camp overnight in the snake pit at the local zoo, while practicing for a violin recital.

like on the inside; we can't tell what people are like by how they look.)

Say: **Some people spend huge amounts of time and money making themselves look good. As Christians, we know it's far more important to develop our inner life with Christ. That's how we can prepare for life in heaven.**

ALIEN DETECTION

Before the meeting, ask three or four people to act as "aliens" in this section of the lesson. Tell them to answer other kids' questions honestly and not to act strangely. Here are some suggestions for producing subtle alien characteristics:

● change the color of their tongues using food coloring;

● put fake moles on their ear lobes using a black water-color marker; or

● have all aliens stand on one foot while talking.

Feel free to use your own ideas for distinguishing your aliens.

Say: **Before we look at how we can live like citizens of heaven on Earth, let's see what we might look like to those who don't know Jesus.**

There are aliens among us! I know because they each have a unique characteristic that sets them apart. Your job is to mingle and talk until you can uncover who among us are from another planet. Go!

After the aliens have been discovered, call everyone together and ask:

● **How did it feel being an alien?** (I knew I was different; I didn't want people to notice what was different about me.)

● **How are these feelings like feelings we sometimes have as Christians in a non-Christian world?** (Sometimes I don't want people to know I'm a Christian; it's hard being different.)

● **What are the distinguishing characteristics that a citizen of heaven on Earth might have?** (She would show love; he would worship God.)

Say: **Heaven is a real place, and all Christians will live there someday. But even while we're here, we're still citizens of heaven. And that means we need to live lives that help others see where we're going. Let's see how we might do that.**

ON EARTH AS IN HEAVEN

Form two groups and give each group a Bible. Assign each group one of these passages: Matthew 6:9-13 and 1 John 3:2-3. Have groups read their passages and decide how the passages apply to living as citizens of heaven now.

Say to the Matthew 6:9-13 group: **Your job is to create a list of ways we can accomplish God's will on Earth in our** daily lives. Write the list on newsprint and tape it to the wall. List things you know are God's will first. For example, to feed the hungry, to stop war, to love your neighbor or to obey your parents. Give this group a sheet of newsprint, a marker and tape.

Say to the 1 John 3:2-3 group: **Your job is to create a poem about your own lives based on the passage. It doesn't have to rhyme or even sound poetic. It just has to explain how the passage relates to the way you live. Title it "Now and Not Yet."** Give this group a sheet of paper and a pencil.

Give groups their supplies and allow them to work for several minutes. Then have them each read their project to the other group.

Ask:

● **Based on what we've seen here, how do Christians live on Earth as citizens of heaven?** (By living according to God's commands; by keeping our eyes focused on Jesus.)

● **What can you do today to live as a citizen of heaven?** (Pray more; tell others about my faith; follow Christ's example.)

Say: **With our new-found knowledge about how we should live, let's do an activity to help bring it all into focus.**

PARADISE PASSPORTS

Form pairs and give kids each a photocopy of the "Passport to Heaven" handout (p. 41), a pencil and a Bible. Have pairs work together to complete their handouts. When pairs are ready, have volunteers share what they wrote on the handout.

Say: **God's gift of eternal life is free. But when we accept it, we need to commit ourselves to serving him because of what he's done for us. And that commitment starts by choosing to live like citizens of heaven while we're still here on Earth.**

If they feel comfortable doing so, have kids sign their names at the bottom of the handout as a sign of their commitment to live "heavenly" lives on Earth.

Have kids form a circle and toss their handouts into the air. Have kids each pick up one handout (not their own) and write on it one way they see that person living like a citizen of heaven here on Earth. Then have kids return the handouts to the owners.

☐ OPTION 1: GOOD INFECTION

Say: **Someone has said Christianity is like a "good disease" that infects people and spreads through them to others through acts of love and kindness. Let's list some ways people could be "infected" by this good disease.**

COMMITMENT
(10 to 15 minutes)

CLOSING
(up to 5 minutes)

On a sheet of newsprint taped to the wall, make four columns, and give each column one of these headings: "Minds," "Hearts," "Hands" and "Feet." Ask kids to brainstorm ways a teenager could be "infected" by Christianity in each of these categories. Then ask kids to brainstorm things that might stop the infection from spreading.

Say: **The population of heaven is always increasing. And when we live as citizens of heaven on Earth, the life Jesus gives us can "infect" others, who then might become citizens of heaven themselves.**

Close with prayer, asking God to help kids live as heaven's citizens on Earth.

☐ OPTION 2: JOINED TOGETHER

Tear a piece of construction paper into a heart-shape. On the heart, write the word "Heaven." Without saying anything, tear off pieces of the heart to give to each person in the room.

After every person has a piece, say: **As citizens of heaven, we each carry a piece of our homeland with us wherever we go. And we need each citizen to do his or her part in life. If just one of you decides not to live as a citizen of heaven, then our heart will have a missing piece. But together, we present a picture of heaven that's hard to ignore.**

Have kids close in silent prayer, asking God to help them live as heaven's citizens here on Earth.

If You Still Have Time . . .

Quotation Discussion—Write the following statement on newsprint: "Happiness is like a butterfly. The more you chase it, the harder it is to catch. But when you focus on other things, it comes and sits gently on your shoulder." Ask:

- What does this quote mean to you?
- How does this quote apply to our discussion of getting to heaven?
- Is getting to heaven more like a goal or a result? Explain.

Course Reflection—Form a circle. Ask students to reflect on the past four lessons. Have them take turns completing the following sentences:

- Something I learned in this course is . . .
- If I could tell my friends about this course, I'd say . . .
- Something I'll do differently because of this course is . . .

PASSPORT to HEAVEN

Name:

Date of birth:

Place of birth:

Date and place of "new birth" (see John 3:3-6):

Are you a foreigner (see Ephesians 2:17-19)? Yes   No
Explain:

State your citizenship (see Philippians 3:20-21):

Current residence:

Future residence (see Psalm 23:6; John 14:2-4):

Kingdom work on Earth:
● My job is to take out the garbage, such as (see Colossians 3:5-9):

● My job also involves dressing myself properly, with (see Colossians 3:12-14):

● Other things I do in Christ's name are (see Colossians 3:15-17):

Possible occupation in heaven (see 2 Timothy 2:12; Revelation 5:10; 22:3-5):

Are you committed to living life on Earth as a citizen of heaven until you die?
Yes   No   Not sure

If yes, sign here: _____

BONUS IDEAS

Bonus Scriptures— The lessons focus on a select few scripture passages, but if you'd like to incorporate more Bible readings into the lessons, here are our suggestions:
- Psalm 15 (The psalmist wonders who may enter God's presence.)
- Isaiah 65:17-25 (Isaiah writes about a new heaven and new Earth.)
- Matthew 6:19-21 (God is more important than money.)
- 2 Corinthians 5:1-10 (Our goal should always be to please God.)
- Philippians 3:17-21 (Follow Christ's example.)
- 1 Thessalonians 4:13-18 (We will be with the Lord forever in heaven.)

Album Cover Critiques— Have a meeting where kids bring heavy metal album covers that deal with hellish themes. Discuss ways popular culture and rock musicians fall short of dealing with the full truth and reality of hell. Consider:
- How do kids generally react to the "scary" aspects of these covers? How much is taken seriously?
- How would you respond to a teenager who feels that listening to hellish music has no affect on his or her moods or attitudes about life?

Pie-in-the Sky?— Give kids each a pencil and a photocopy of the "Is Heaven Just Pie-in-the-Sky?" handout (p. 46). Have volunteers read each point of view aloud, and then give kids time to respond to the two questions. After a few minutes, ask for kids' responses and move into a discussion about whether it is "proper" to look forward to a heavenly reward.

Field Trip— Plan a trip to a local planetarium to help kids learn about the physical heavens. In a debriefing session, ask:
- **What feelings did you have when viewing the awesomeness of space and its stars and planets? Did you have any thoughts about God? Explain.**
- **In what ways does the existence and majesty of the physical heavens affect your view of a future heavenly existence?**

I Swear!— Ask your students how many kids at their school they would guess have used the word "hell" as a swear word. Tell kids hell is a biblical, theological word. Then ask:
- **Why do you think this word is so often used in cursing?**

MEETINGS AND MORE

● **Do you think talking about the reality of hell could scare someone into becoming a Christian? Why or why not?**

Musical Heaven— Hold a discussion of heaven based on views of heaven presented in music. Have kids bring tapes of Christian and secular songs about heaven. Also bring songs you find. Some you might want to discuss are "Stairway to Heaven" by Led Zeppelin, "Heaven Is a Real Place" by Charlie Peacock and "Heaven" by BeBe and CeCe Winans. Search for bits of truth in the songs as well as for falsehoods.

Table Talk— Use the "Table Talk" handout (p. 19) as the basis for a meeting with parents and teenagers. During the meeting, have parents and kids complete the handout and discuss it. For a twist, hold the meeting outdoors in front of a blazing bonfire and talk about any correlations kids and parents feel between the fire and hell. Roast hot dogs and marshmallows for fun!

PARTY PLEASERS

Heaven and Hell Mixer— Have two different rooms (or two different locations) decorated as heaven (a bright, cloud theme) and hell (a dark, fiery theme). Kids could design and wear costumes appropriate to the room or location where they were sent by individual invitation. After initial, separate and mixer activities, bring both the heavenly and hellish groups together for a discussion about how people actually end up in either place. Use the opportunity to give a clear presentation of God's plan for giving us eternal life in heaven.

Hot or Cold— Have a pool party at a place where there's also a sauna. Be sure all your kids at least step into the hot sauna to see what it's like. Take a break in the party to discuss ways the sauna might be similar to hell and ways the pool might be similar to heaven.

RETREAT IDEA

Heaven or Hell— Hold a retreat in two parts: the first based on hell and the second based on heaven. For the first hour of the retreat, forbid any interaction among group members. No one is to do anything with anyone else. Everyone, including you, must keep completely silent. Your communication with the group should be minimal and should be done only through written signs.

After the hour is up, call an end to "hell" and discuss the

experience. Then move on to "heaven," having lots of fellowship, celebration and worship. At the end of your retreat, debrief the heaven experience and have kids compare the two. Be sure to emphasize both of the experiences were extremely weak representations of what the real things would be like.

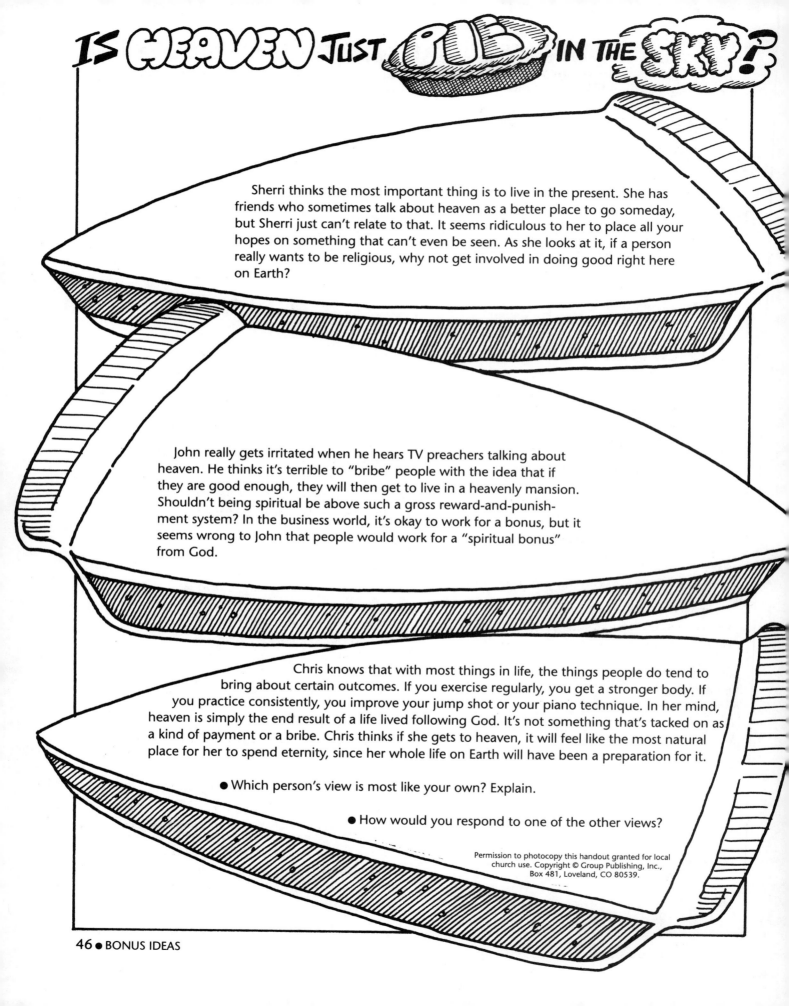

IS HEAVEN JUST PIE IN THE SKY?

Sherri thinks the most important thing is to live in the present. She has friends who sometimes talk about heaven as a better place to go someday, but Sherri just can't relate to that. It seems ridiculous to her to place all your hopes on something that can't even be seen. As she looks at it, if a person really wants to be religious, why not get involved in doing good right here on Earth?

John really gets irritated when he hears TV preachers talking about heaven. He thinks it's terrible to "bribe" people with the idea that if they are good enough, they will then get to live in a heavenly mansion. Shouldn't being spiritual be above such a gross reward-and-punishment system? In the business world, it's okay to work for a bonus, but it seems wrong to John that people would work for a "spiritual bonus" from God.

Chris knows that with most things in life, the things people do tend to bring about certain outcomes. If you exercise regularly, you get a stronger body. If you practice consistently, you improve your jump shot or your piano technique. In her mind, heaven is simply the end result of a life lived following God. It's not something that's tacked on as a kind of payment or a bribe. Chris thinks if she gets to heaven, it will feel like the most natural place for her to spend eternity, since her whole life on Earth will have been a preparation for it.

● Which person's view is most like your own? Explain.

● How would you respond to one of the other views?

CURRICULUM REORDER—TOP PRIORITY

Order now to prepare for your upcoming Sunday school classes, youth ministry meetings, and weekend retreats! Each book includes all teacher and student materials—plus photo-copiable handouts—for any size class . . . for just $8.99 each!

FOR SENIOR HIGH:

1 & 2 Corinthians: Christian Discipleship, ISBN 1-55945-230-7

Angels, Demons, Miracles & Prayer, ISBN 1-55945-235-8

Changing the World, ISBN 1-55945-236-6

Christians in a Non-Christian World, ISBN 1-55945-224-2

Christlike Leadership, ISBN 1-55945-231-5

Communicating With Friends, ISBN 1-55945-228-5

Counterfeit Religions, ISBN 1-55945-207-2

Dating Decisions, ISBN 1-55945-215-3

Dealing With Life's Pressures, ISBN 1-55945-232-3

Deciphering Jesus' Parables, ISBN 1-55945-237-4

Exodus: Following God, ISBN 1-55945-226-9

Exploring Ethical Issues, ISBN 1-55945-225-0

Faith for Tough Times, ISBN 1-55945-216-1

Forgiveness, ISBN 1-55945-223-4

Getting Along With Parents, ISBN 1-55945-202-1

Getting Along With Your Family, ISBN 1-55945-233-1

The Gospel of John: Jesus' Teachings, ISBN 1-55945-208-0

Hazardous to Your Health: AIDS, Steroids & Eating Disorders, ISBN 1-55945-200-5

Is Marriage in Your Future?, ISBN 1-55945-203-X

Jesus' Death & Resurrection, ISBN 1-55945-211-0

The Joy of Serving, ISBN 1-55945-210-2

Knowing God's Will, ISBN 1-55945-205-6

Life After High School, ISBN 1-55945-220-X

Making Good Decisions, ISBN 1-55945-209-9

Money: A Christian Perspective, ISBN 1-55945-212-9

Movies, Music, TV & Me, ISBN 1-55945-213-7

Overcoming Insecurities, ISBN 1-55945-221-8

Psalms, ISBN 1-55945-234-X

Real People, Real Faith: Amy Grant, Joni Eareckson Tada, Dave Dravecky, Terry Anderson, ISBN 1-55945-238-2

Responding to Injustice, ISBN 1-55945-214-5

Revelation, ISBN 1-55945-229-3

School Struggles, ISBN 1-55945-201-3

Sex: A Christian Perspective, ISBN 1-55945-206-4

Today's Lessons From Yesterday's Prophets, ISBN 1-55945-227-7

Turning Depression Upside Down, ISBN 1-55945-135-1

What Is the Church?, ISBN 1-55945-222-6

Who Is God?, ISBN 1-55945-218-8

Who Is Jesus?, ISBN 1-55945-219-6

Who Is the Holy Spirit?, ISBN 1-55945-217-X

Your Life as a Disciple, ISBN 1-55945-204-8

FOR JUNIOR HIGH/MIDDLE SCHOOL:

Accepting Others: Beyond Barriers & Stereotypes, ISBN 1-55945-126-2

Advice to Young Christians: Exploring Paul's Letters, ISBN 1-55945-146-7

Applying the Bible to Life, ISBN 1-55945-116-5

Becoming Responsible, ISBN 1-55945-109-2

Bible Heroes: Joseph, Esther, Mary & Peter, ISBN 1-55945-137-8

Boosting Self-Esteem, ISBN 1-55945-100-9

Building Better Friendships, ISBN 1-55945-138-6

Can Christians Have Fun?, ISBN 1-55945-134-3

Caring for God's Creation, ISBN 1-55945-121-1

Christmas: A Fresh Look, ISBN 1-55945-124-6

Competition, ISBN 1-55945-133-5

Dealing With Death, ISBN 1-55945-112-2

Dealing With Disappointment, ISBN 1-55945-139-4

Doing Your Best, ISBN 1-55945-142-4

Drugs & Drinking, ISBN 1-55945-118-1

Evil and the Occult, ISBN 1-55945-102-5

Genesis: The Beginnings, ISBN 1-55945-111-4

Guys & Girls: Understanding Each Other, ISBN 1-55945-110-6

Handling Conflict, ISBN 1-55945-125-4

Heaven & Hell, ISBN 1-55945-131-9

Is God Unfair?, ISBN 1-55945-108-4

Love or Infatuation?, ISBN 1-55945-128-9

Making Parents Proud, ISBN 1-55945-107-6

Making the Most of School, ISBN 1-55945-113-0

Materialism, ISBN 1-55945-130-0

The Miracle of Easter, ISBN 1-55945-143-2

Miracles!, ISBN 1-55945-117-3

Peace & War, ISBN 1-55945-123-8

Peer Pressure, ISBN 1-55945-103-3

Prayer, ISBN 1-55945-104-1

Reaching Out to a Hurting World, ISBN 1-55945-140-8

Sermon on the Mount, ISBN 1-55945-129-7

Suicide: The Silent Epidemic, ISBN 1-55945-145-9

Telling Your Friends About Christ, ISBN 1-55945-114-9

The Ten Commandments, ISBN 1-55945-127-0

Today's Faith Heroes: Madeline Manning Mims, Michael W. Smith, Mother Teresa, Bruce Olson, ISBN 1-55945-141-6

Today's Media: Choosing Wisely, ISBN 1-55945-144-0

Today's Music: Good or Bad?, ISBN 1-55945-101-7

What Is God's Purpose for Me?, ISBN 1-55945-132-7

What's a Christian?, ISBN 1-55945-105-X

Order today from your local Christian bookstore, or write: Group Publishing, Box 485, Loveland, CO 80539. For mail orders, please add postage/handling of $4 for orders up to $15, $5 for orders of $15.01+. Colorado residents add 3% sales tax.

MORE PROGRAMMING IDEAS FOR YOUR ACTIVE GROUP...

DO IT! ACTIVE LEARNING IN YOUTH MINISTRY

Thom and Joani Schultz

Discover the keys to teaching creative faith-building lessons that teenagers look forward to...and remember for a lifetime. You'll learn how to design simple, fun programs that will help your kids...

- build community,
- develop communication skills,
- relate better to others,
- experience what it's really like to be a Christian,

...and apply the Bible to their daily challenges. Plus, you'll get 24 ready-to-use active-learning exercises complete with debriefing questions and Bible application. For example, your kids will...

- learn the importance of teamwork and the value of each team member by juggling six different objects as a group,
- experience community and God's grace using a doughnut,
- grow more sensitive to others' needs by acting out Matthew 25:31-46

...just to name a few. And the practical index of over 30 active-learning resources will make your planning easier.

ISBN 0-931529-94-8

DEVOTIONS FOR YOUTH GROUPS ON THE GO

Dan and Cindy Hansen

Now it's easy to turn every youth group trip into an opportunity for spiritual growth for your kids. This resource gives you 52 easy-to-prepare devotions that teach meaningful spiritual lessons using the experiences of your group's favorite outings. You'll get devotions perfect for everything from amusement parks, to choir trips, to miniature golf, to the zoo. Your kids will gain new insights from the Bible as they...

- discuss how many "strikes" God gives us—after enjoying a game of softball,
- experience the hardship of Jesus' temptation in the wilderness—on a camping trip,
- understand the disciples' relief when Jesus calmed the storm—while white-water rafting, even

...learn to trust God's will when bad weather cancels an event or the bus breaks down!

Plus, the handy topical listing makes your planning easy.

ISBN 1-55945-075-4